Grief is a Team Sport

What Every Griever and Their Team

Needs to Know

By

Dr. Fred Batten, Jr.

Watersprings
PUBLISHING

Grief is a Team Sport, published by Watersprings Publishing,
a division of Watersprings Media House, LLC.

P.O. Box 1284 Olive Branch, MS 38654

www.waterspringspublishing.com

Contact the publisher for bulk orders and permission requests.

Printed in the United States of America.

ISBN-13: 978-1-964972-15-2

DEDICATION

To Denise,

My beloved wife and faithful teammate in life and in grief. Your love steadied me when the ground shifted. Your steady strength, unwavering support, and grace gave me space to write, reflect, and heal. Thank you for walking this journey beside me—not just as my partner in life, but as my teammate in grief and healing. This book bears the imprint of your faithfulness.

To Amber and Brandi,

My daughters, my joy, and my inspiration.

Thank you for your compassion, patience, and encouragement. You remind me daily that love endures beyond loss, and that hope can be passed down through generations.

To the trusted readers and friends who walked with me through early drafts, Your honest insights, thoughtful feedback, and generous spirit sharpened the message and deepened the impact of these pages. Your contributions will continue to bless many.

And to the cherished memory of my brother,

Ernest Bowen (1962–2021)

Your life, love, and loss gave birth to this book.

Though your absence is deeply felt, your presence lives on in every chapter. May your memory continue to guide and comfort all who grieve. This is for you.

CONTENTS

GRIEF, LIKE FOOTBALL, REQUIRES THE RIGHT FORMATION TO MOVE FORWARD.

INTRODUCTION
GRIEF IS A TEAM SPORT

As a pastor and chaplain, I've spent decades walking alongside individuals and families in their darkest moments—offering prayers, comfort, and presence as they faced unimaginable loss. I thought I understood grief. But it wasn't until I lost my own brother, Ernest, that grief became personal. Suddenly, I wasn't the helper, I was the one hurting. It was then that I truly began to understand the depth of emotional pain, the importance of emotional intelligence, and the power of letting others help carry the load.

Grief is a Team Sport was born from that experience.

This book is for the grieving—and for those who care about them. Whether you're navigating your own journey through loss or trying to support someone who is, this guide offers insights, encouragement, and practical tools for healing with compassion and community. Grieving doesn't have to be done alone. In fact, it shouldn't be.

I invite you to use the companion workbook as well—a hands-on resource designed to help you or your team move intentionally and intelligently through the healing process. Together, they form a roadmap toward hope, resilience, and wholeness.

You're not alone. Let the team help.

Dr. Fred Batten, Jr.

FOREWORD

Grief is an evolving reminder that we can love…have loved…beyond our wildest dreams!

I first met Dr. Batten during his service as a minister in Jackson, Mississippi. He came quietly, unassuming, but with a fan base of family, friends, and former congregants who filled our pews to accompany him to his introductory service. Where most new pastors showed up with their wives, children, and a bible, Dr. Batten had all that AND a posse!

We soon learned why he was so adored! He was articulate, intelligent, honest, and kind - a wordsmith who spoke thoughtfully and with a heart of care and love. "Grief is a Team Sport" skillfully captures Dr. Batten's talent and ability to frame the human experience - especially the natural process of grief. The care and sensitivity needed for such a complex topic are expertly weaved through a text of playful analogies, psychological research, theory, and spiritual precision.

"Grief is a Team Sport" is for the reader in need of a measured voice among the noise - one that makes sense of the chaos swirling in the human heart and mind following an intimate loss. The paradoxical experience of what feels thunderously loud and breathtakingly still, unbelievably illusive yet painfully real is unpacked and explained for the normality it is - grief!

If you've loved and lost, remember you were blessed with a love beyond your wildest dreams!

Happy reading!

Dr. Jemika Michael Simmons,

Educator, Grief Survivor, First Lady of Greenville, MS

Chapter 1:

THE OPENING KICKOFF – UNDERSTANDING GRIEF AS A TEAM EXPERIENCE

The stadium buzzed with anticipation as the special teams lined up for the kickoff. This wasn't just any game; it was the dawn of a new era in the NFL. With the league's latest rule change, kickoffs would now look drastically different. No more full-speed collisions from players sprinting downfield like missiles. Instead, teams had to be in their proper places before the ball was kicked, a move designed to reduce injuries and make the players safer. Some players appreciated the effort to prolong their careers, while others grumbled that it took away the thrill of the game. Fans were divided, too. Some missed the high-speed drama, while others welcomed a safer approach that kept their favorite athletes on the field longer. Regardless of opinion, one thing was clear: the NFL was evolving, and teams had to adapt.

Grief, like football, requires the right formation to move forward. Just as a team must be properly positioned before the kickoff, a grieving person needs to surround themselves with the right support to begin the healing journey. No one wins a football game alone, and no one navigates grief in isolation. The people around you, family, friends, counselors, and support groups, become your blockers, shielding you from unnecessary pain while helping you push through the toughest moments. Without the right team, the weight of loss can feel unbearable. But with the right people in place, healing, like a well-executed play, becomes possible.

The moment the phone rang, David felt his stomach tighten. He already knew what was coming. His father's long battle with cancer was nearing its end, and every call from the hospital felt like a countdown. Chaplain Ray Giunta once said, *"Grief is a journey, not a destination."* David was already on that road, though his father was still alive. This was *anticipatory grief,* the pain of knowing loss is coming before it happens. He found himself grieving in advance, mourning the conversations they wouldn't have, the moments his father wouldn't witness. It was like standing on the sidelines before the game started, knowing the final score was already set.

After the funeral, David expected grief to loosen its grip, but weeks turned into months, and the weight didn't lift. His pain wasn't just lingering. It was growing heavier. Dr. Alan D. Wolfelt describes this as *prolonged grief,* when sorrow stretches far beyond the expected mourning period, making it difficult to function. He writes, *"Mourning never really ends. Only as time goes on, it erupts less frequently."* But for David, the eruptions were relentless. He struggled to concentrate at work, withdrew from friends, and felt trapped in his sorrow. His teammates in life—his family, his friends—wanted him to move forward, but he was stuck at the line of scrimmage, unable to make the next play.

Grief doesn't always fit into society's expectations. Here's an example. When Larissa lost her ex-husband, people offered little sympathy. They had divorced years ago, so why was she so heartbroken? What they didn't understand was that love, even more complicated, doesn't simply vanish. Dr. Elisabeth Kübler-Ross, who pioneered the five stages of grief, once wrote, "The reality is that you will grieve forever. You will not 'get over' the loss of a loved one; you will learn to live with it." Lisa's grief wasn't openly acknowledged, making it *disenfranchised grief*—a loss that isn't publicly validated. She felt isolated, as though she had no right to mourn. In football terms, it was like playing without a team, hurting, but with no one recognizing the injury.

Sometimes the momentum of the game changes with multiple turnovers, like a fumble, an interception, or a muffed punt. For Michael, grief didn't come from one loss, but many. First, his brother died in a car accident. A year later, his best friend passed suddenly. Then, his mother was diagnosed with Alzheimer's. Each loss compounded the next, making it hard to separate one from the other. This was *cumulative grief*, where multiple losses piled up, leaving little time to process before the next blow comes. It's like a team suffering injury after injury, never given a chance to recover before another player goes down. Grief, when unrelenting, can feel like a season with no off days, no timeouts, no halftime break to regroup.

Many people use *grief, mourning*, and *bereavement* interchangeably, but they aren't the same. *Bereavement* is the state of loss itself, the reality of having someone taken, ripped away. *Grief* is the internal response, the emotions that swirl in its aftermath. *Mourning*, on the other hand, is what we do with our grief, the outward expressions, like funerals, rituals, or even something as simple as lighting a candle in remembrance. Dr. Wolfelt explains, "Grief is what's inside you. Mourning is what you do with it." Just like football requires both strategy and execution, healing requires both feeling and expression.

In grief, as in football, the right team makes all the difference. Some losses, like terminal illness, come with time to prepare. Others hit suddenly, leaving us breathless and broken. Some grief is invisible to others, while for some, grief keeps coming, wave after wave. But no matter how grief arrives, no one should go through it alone. Healing is not a solo sport. It takes a team—one that requires support, patience, and the courage to keep moving forward, even when the game feels impossible to win, to heal.

Again, like football, grief has both individual and team components. A running back carries the ball alone, maneuvering through obstacles, but without the offensive line blocking and creating space, every run would be stopped in its tracks. In the same way, *personal grief* is the unique, internal experience of loss—how an individual processes pain, memories, and emotions. Each person grieves differently, based on their personality, experiences, and faith. Yet, grief is not meant to be carried alone. *Communal grief* is the shared response—how family, friends, and even society come together to support the grieving. Dr. Alan D. Wolfelt explains, "When words are inadequate, have a ritual." Funerals, memorial services, and gatherings of support exist because grief is both a personal and communal experience. Without that balance, healing is much harder to achieve.

Motivational speaker Les Brown once said, "Ask for help not because you're weak, but because you want to remain strong." This reflects the biblical principle found in Galatians 6:2, "Bear ye one another's burdens, and so fulfill the law of Christ." While personal grief is unavoidable—no one else can feel your loss for you—communal grief ensures that no one walks through sorrow alone. The disciples grieved individually when Jesus was crucified, each struggling with doubt and fear. Still, it was in their gathering together in the Upper Room that they found strength (Acts 1:14). Just as a football team regroups after a tough loss, the grieving need the presence of others to lift them, remind them of hope, and create pathways for healing.

One faith writer speaks to this need for communal support in *The Ministry of Healing*, writing, "In the path which He had marked out for us, He had given us the privilege of sharing in the work of relieving human suffering." This is the essence of communal grief, when others step in to help carry the weight. Yet, just as an offensive line can't run the ball, no one can grieve on behalf of another. The grieving individual must do the internal work of acknowledging pain, finding meaning, and taking steps toward healing. The key is connection. When the running back trusts his team and the team works in sync, the play moves forward. When an individual leans into the right community, one that listens, prays, and encourages, the healing process gains momentum.

Even Jesus demonstrated the balance between personal and communal grief. In John 11:35, "Jesus wept." He experienced the deep, personal sorrow of losing His friend Lazarus. But He didn't grieve alone. Mary, Martha, and the gathered mourners shared in the loss. Ultimately, Jesus provided hope by resurrecting Lazarus, showing that grief is not the final chapter. As in football, success comes from both individual skill and teamwork. Grief is no different. Healing begins personally but is sustained through community. The question is, who is doing the blocking for you as you carry the weight of your loss?

Grief, though deeply personal, is never meant to be faced alone. *"No man is an island,"* wrote John Donne, reminding us that human suffering, like human joy, is best carried in the presence of others. Dr. Alan D. Wolfelt affirms that healing in grief is not about 'getting over it' but about learning to reconcile with it, with the love and support of others. Even the Bible reinforces this truth in Ecclesiastes 4:9-10, "Two are better than one… if either of them falls, one can help the other up." Motivational speaker Tony Robbins echoes this sentiment: "The quality of your life is the quality of your relationships," because in loss, it is the people around us who become our safety net. Ellen White expands on this in *The Desire of Ages*, writing, "In our sorrow, Christ sends His angels to comfort us, often through the presence of fellow believers who uplift and strengthen." Similarly, Dr. Elisabeth Kübler-Ross observed, "The reality is that you will grieve forever. You will not 'get over' the loss of a loved one; you will learn to live with it, and you will heal by reaching out and allowing others to walk the journey with you." Like a football team protecting its quarterback, grief requires the right formation of support—people who block out isolation, tackle despair, and push forward with encouragement. Even Jesus, in His moment of sorrow in Gethsemane, sought the company of Peter, James, and John (Matthew 26:37-38), showing us that even the strongest need companionship in suffering. Grief is shouldering sorrow together; it is a journey meant to be traveled together, with others standing beside us, carrying the weight when we can't, and reminding us that healing, though slow, is possible.

I was sitting in my home office in Fort Lauderdale, Florida, when the call came. My brother, Ernest—Ernie—was gone. In that hospital room in Murfreesboro, Tennessee, far from where I sat, COVID took him, and yet the weight of his absence crushed me instantly. My heart ached in ways I had never known. I cried hard. Clinging to my wife, the waves of sorrow and disbelief swept over me. For days, confusion clouded my mind. How could Ernie be gone? He had always been my elementary school defender, my rescuer. The one who turned Tommy Climber inside out for roughing me up while playing king of the mountain. The one who coaxed me onto my first horse. The one who could fix anything, from broken appliances to broken spirits. And now, the one thing none of us could fix was the emptiness he left behind. And I am so grateful for my support; my wife and daughters, family, friends, pastors, and fellow chaplains who were important to my healing and recovery. While everyone may not swiftly march down the field, recovery "is that time when we begin to move forward into life again, journeying on the path to discovering new feelings and new understandings about ourselves and our loss" (Giunta, 2002).

REFERENCE LIST

Donne, J. (1624). *Devotions upon emergent occasions*. London: Printed by A.M.

Giunta, R. (2002). *The grief recovery workbook: helping you weather the storm of loss and overwhelming disappointment*. Harper Christian Resources.

Kübler-Ross, E., & Kessler, D. (2005). *On grief and grieving: Finding the meaning of grief through the five stages of loss*. Scribner.

Robbins, T. (n.d.). [Quote]. Retrieved from https://www.tonyrobbins.com

The Holy Bible, King James Version. (n.d.). Thomas Nelson.

White, E. G. (1905). *The Ministry of Healing*. Pacific Press Publishing Association.

White, E. G. (1898). *The Desire of Ages*. Pacific Press Publishing Association.

Wolfelt, A. D. (2004). *Understanding your grief: Ten essential touchstones for finding hope and healing your heart*. Companion Press.

Wolfelt, A. D. (2005). *Companioning the bereaved: A soulful guide for counselors and caregivers*. Companion Press.

Giunta, R. (2004). *Grief Recovery: A Biblical Healing Guide*. Warner Faith.

Brown, L. (n.d.). [Quote]. Retrieved from https://lesbrown.com

Chapter 2:

THE MYTHS WE CARRY

Michael Jordan wasn't cut from his high school basketball team—at least, not in the way most people tell it. But somewhere along the way, that story became gospel: Jordan, humiliated, sent home, told he wasn't good enough. It's a tidy story, one that wraps struggle in triumph and sells resilience like a jersey. The truth? He was a sophomore who didn't make varsity and got placed on JV instead—a normal coaching decision. Yet we love the myth more than the messy, nuanced truth. It's more dramatic. More emotional. More marketable. Grief works the same way. Somewhere between loss and healing, myths form stories we tell ourselves or inherit from others. But if we're ever going to move forward, we must start by separating what's legendary from what's real.

They called it the Curse of the Bambino—an 86-year drought of failure, all blamed on a single trade. Babe Ruth, sold to the Yankees, took the Boston Red Sox's winning spirit with him, or so the story went. For generations, fans believed a curse—not missed fly balls, bad pitching, or poor management—was the reason their team couldn't win. It became a blanket for disappointment, a myth so powerful it shaped the culture of an entire city. But the truth was far less magical and far more human. In grief, we do this too. We cling to myths to explain our pain, believing that if we find the right narrative, the ache will make sense. But real healing doesn't come from legends. It comes from facing the raw, often unglamorous truth—together.

They say women grieve more than men. You've heard it. Maybe even said it. She cried more, she talked about it more, so she must feel it more deeply. But the truth is, men and women grieve differently, not more or

15

less. Researchers from the American Psychological Association note that men often express grief through action, such as fixing things, working, running, or going silent, rather than through tears. The myth persists because our culture tends to associate visible emotion with validity. I didn't cry much when my grandfather died. But years later, writing *Wisdom from Generation 2 Generation*, I felt his presence in every line, his voice in every sentence. Grief was there all along, quiet, steady, sacred. It wasn't loud, but it was real. And writing became my way of weeping and honoring him all over again.

Another myth? Grief happens in a straight line. We often hear about the "five stages of grief" like they're a checklist: denial, anger, bargaining, depression, acceptance. But the model—originally intended for people facing terminal illness, not necessarily those left behind—has been misapplied and misunderstood. A 2007 study published in *JAMA* revealed that grief rarely unfolds in a neat sequence. It's more like a storm pattern, unpredictable, swirling, looping back on itself. Some days you accept it; the next, you're bargaining with God all over again. When I was editing *Wisdom from Generation 2 Generation*, I laughed at my grandfather's sayings, then I sat in silence at what I'd never get to ask him. I wasn't moving in a line—I was moving through love, memory, and longing. And that movement is still in progress.

Then there's this: "Time heals all wounds." It sounds beautiful. Clean. Hopeful. But in truth, time by itself does nothing. It's what we do with the time that matters. Harvard psychologist George Bonanno's work on bereavement shows that people who actively engage in meaning-making activities such as journaling, storytelling, serving others—process grief more healthily than those who simply wait it out. Writing *Wisdom from Generation 2 Generation* wasn't a waiting room. It was a workshop. Every story I recalled, every proverb I unearthed, was a stitch in my soul's mending. Time didn't heal me. Truth did. And writing helped me face it.

Many believe grief has an endpoint—that if you're still mourning years later, something's wrong. But as author Megan Devine writes in her book, *It's OK that You're Not OK: Meeting Grief and Loss in a Culture that Doesn't Understand*, "Some things cannot be fixed. They can only be carried" *(2017)*. Grief doesn't end. It evolves. We integrate it into our lives like scar tissue—stronger, sensitive, always part of us. There are days when I still reach for the phone to call my grandfather. There are moments when his silence feels like thunder. And yet, in every story I pass on, in every young man I mentor with his same grit, I carry him forward. That isn't unfinished grief. It's faithful remembrance.

In a culture that prizes strength and stoicism, grief is often mislabeled as a weakness. But expressing grief isn't a weakness, it's a witness. It says, "This person mattered." In Scripture, even Jesus wept (John 11:35). And in His tears at Lazarus' tomb, we see not frailty but holy empathy. Mental health professionals affirm that those who embrace and express their grief are often more emotionally resilient in the long run. When I opened up through my writing—through remembering my grandfather's laughter, his phrases, his pauses—I found not a crack in my armor, but a new kind of strength. The kind that comes from being human.

C.S. Lewis once said, "No one ever told me that grief felt so like fear." Author Megan Devine wrote, "Some things cannot be fixed. They can only be carried." And Jesus Himself promised, "Blessed are those who mourn, for they shall be comforted" (Matthew 5:4). Grief myths keep us isolated, trapped in silence, shame, and confusion. But the truth sets us free. Free to feel. Free to remember. Free to grieve in community. Free to carry our sorrow and still move forward. Loss is shared and so is recovery—and when we let others into our process, when we invite wisdom, stories, and Sacred texts into our sorrow, we begin to heal not by forgetting, but by remembering rightly.

REFERENCE LIST

American Psychological Association. (2011). *Men and stress: Men's health month.* https://www.apa.org/news/press/releases/stress/2011/mens-health

Bonanno, G. A. (2009). *The other side of sadness: What the new science of bereavement tells us about life after loss.* Basic Books.

Devine, M. (2017). *It's OK that you're not OK: Meeting grief and loss in a culture that doesn't understand.* Sounds True.

Maciejewski, P. K., Zhang, B., Block, S. D., & Prigerson, H. G. (2007). An empirical examination of the stage theory of grief. *JAMA, 297*(7), 716–723. https://doi.org/10.1001/jama.297.7.716

The Holy Bible, New International Version. (2011). Biblica, Inc. (Original work published 1978)

Batten, F., Jr. (n.d.). *Wisdom from Generation 2 Generation.* [Self-published].

Chapter 3:

THE PLAYBOOK – CULTURAL PERSPECTIVES ON GRIEF

The Detroit Pistons of the late 1980s didn't just play basketball; they imposed their will. The "Bad Boys" bruised and battered opponents, turning every game into a war of attrition. Their strategy was simple: relentless defense, hard fouls, and a toughness that tested the mental and physical endurance of anyone daring to challenge them. Meanwhile, the Showtime Lakers ran the floor with elegance, dazzling fans with no-look passes and fast breaks that felt like art in motion. Two teams, two styles—one defined by grit, the other by grace. The way teams approached the game mirrored their identity, just like the way people process grief is shaped by culture, upbringing, and experience. Some fight through pain with resilience forged in hardship; others lean on the support of those around them, finding strength in connection.

Today's NBA is a different world, with less hand-checking, fewer brawls, and more space to operate. Three-pointers fly with a frequency unthinkable in the '80s, where big men battled for rebounds and mid-range jumpers ruled the scoreboard. Just as the game has evolved, so has the way we deal with loss. Some cultures still believe in the old-school toughness, suppressing emotions, pushing through, believing that grief is a private battle. Others embrace a more open style, sharing memories, seeking therapy, and creating space for healing. But whether in basketball or in grief, one truth remains: you don't win alone. The best teams, and the strongest mourners, understand that survival, whether through a seven-game series or the loss of a loved one, is always a team effort.

When David lost his father, his grief followed a familiar script. His family held a simple memorial service—white roses on a polished casket, a slideshow of cherished memories, and a eulogy that spoke more of celebration than sorrow. At the reception, guests exchanged quiet condolences over coffee and sandwiches before heading home, each carrying their grief in their own way. In many Caucasian communities, grief is a personal journey, something to be processed internally or with the help of professionals. Studies show that White Americans are more likely to seek therapy for grief compared to other racial groups. According to the National Center for Health Statistics (2021), White Americans utilize mental health services at nearly twice the rate of Black and Hispanic Americans, a reflection of cultural norms that encourage professional intervention rather than communal grieving.

This preference for an individualized approach can be seen in the way many navigate loss. Grief counseling, self-help books, and support groups are common outlets. A study by Neimeyer et al. (2014) found that White Americans are more likely to engage in cognitive-based coping strategies—talk therapy, journaling, and structured grief programs—rather than spiritual or extended communal rituals. For David, booking an appointment with a grief counselor felt as natural as visiting a doctor for a physical check-up. "You process it, you move forward," he told a friend. There was no expectation of prolonged mourning, no need for public displays of sorrow. His father had lived a full life, and now it was time to honor him by carrying on.

Even the structure of memorial services in many Caucasian communities reflects this straightforward approach. Funerals tend to be brief, formal, and focused on closure. Unlike cultures where grief is displayed openly for weeks, many White American families prefer subdued, efficient ceremonies, often with cremation as a popular choice. According to the National Funeral Directors Association (2022), cremation rates among White Americans reached nearly 75%, compared to significantly lower rates among Black and Hispanic populations, where traditional burials and extended mourning periods remain more common. The emphasis is on remembering life, not lingering in loss.

Yet, while the process is often more private, it does not mean grief is absent. It simply takes a different form, one that values independence, personal reflection, and controlled expression. For David, healing didn't come in wailing or ritual; it came in quiet moments of remembrance, in long drives with his father's favorite music playing, in conversations with a therapist who helped him find meaning in the pain. His grief wasn't displayed for all to see, but it was still deeply felt—proving that even when grief seems solitary, it still requires a team, whether made up of close friends, professionals, or the quiet strength of memories that refuse to fade.

When Maria's grandmother passed away, grief did not belong to her alone. It belonged to the entire family. In the days following the funeral, a steady stream of relatives arrived at her home, bringing tamales, warm embraces, and shared memories. No one mourned in isolation. The loss was felt as a collective, and the healing would happen together. This deep sense of familial grieving is woven into Hispanic culture, where mourning is not just an individual process but a communal one, rooted in centuries-old traditions. Studies show that Hispanic families tend to emphasize family support in bereavement. According to Pew Research (2021), Hispanic Americans are more likely than White Americans to rely on extended family and religious communities during times of loss, seeing grief as a shared burden rather than a private struggle.

One of the most enduring grief traditions in Hispanic culture is the Novena, nine days of prayer following a loved one's death. Each evening, Maria's family gathered in her grandmother's home, lighting candles and reciting prayers, their voices blending in reverence. Research from the Journal of Palliative Medicine (2018) highlights how such rituals provide emotional and spiritual comfort, reinforcing familial bonds and a sense of continuity between the living and the dead. The Novena was not just about prayer; it was a time for storytelling, for laughter through tears, for meals prepared together as a way of honoring the one they lost. It was grief made visible, a shared act of remembrance that held them together.

Even beyond the funeral and Novena, grief remained an active part of life. Every November 1st, Maria's family, like millions across Latin America and the United States, celebrated Día de los Muertos—The Day of the Dead. A small altar, or *ofrenda*, was built in their home, decorated with marigolds, sugar skulls, and a framed photo of her grandmother. A plate of her favorite food sat next to a candle, a symbol of welcome for her spirit. Unlike the somberness of many Western grief traditions, Día de los Muertos is a vibrant, colorful celebration, reinforcing the belief that death is not an end, but a transition. A study from the American Journal of Cultural Sociology (2020) found that Hispanic families are more likely to engage in ongoing commemorative rituals for their deceased loved ones, integrating their memories into daily life rather than compartmentalizing grief.

For Maria, this way of grieving felt natural. The presence of her grandmother lingered, not just in the photographs and traditions, but in the way her family came together, in the stories passed down, in the meals cooked with her recipes. Grief in her culture was not something to be shouldered alone; it was a thread that wove the family even tighter. In this way, Maria learned that healing wasn't about moving on. It was about carrying forward, surrounded by the love and support of her team.

When James lost his mother, grief did not whisper—it sang, it shouted, it filled the sanctuary with the sound of voices lifted in sorrow and celebration. The funeral was not just a ceremony but a communal event, held in the same church where his mother had prayed, where she had ushered during worship services, and where she had sung hymns that now carried new weight. In African American culture, grief is not a solitary burden; it is carried together, shaped by the church, by history, by a collective resilience born from struggle. Dr. Michael Eric Dyson, in *Tears We Cannot Stop* (2017), describes how Black funerals are both sacred and social spaces where pain is poured out in testimony, music, and movement. Here, grief is not contained; it is expressed in full, a catharsis that binds the community together.

The Black church has long been the cornerstone of African American grief rituals. Howard Thurman, in *Deep River and The Negro Spiritual Speaks of Life and Death*, explains how the spirituals of enslaved Africans transformed sorrow into strength, creating a theology of survival that persists in Black churches today. At James's mother's funeral, the choir did not sing quietly—they sang with conviction, their voices swelling like waves, lifting the congregation in both mourning and hope. The preacher did not simply read a scripture; he called the family to "weep if you must but know that joy comes in the morning." Funerals in the Black community are more than farewells—they are transitions, celebrations of a life well-lived and a soul returning to God. Research from the Journal of Black Studies (2020) affirms that expressive memorial services, often marked by call-and-response, gospel music, and eulogies that blend grief with gratitude, serve as a vital coping mechanism in African American bereavement.

Beyond the funeral, grief continues in the embrace of the church and the wider community. Meals are prepared, stories are shared, and anniversaries of loss are acknowledged in family gatherings and church services. Mourning is extended, not rushed. James found himself surrounded by women from the church who called to check on him, deacons who dropped by unannounced to pray, and friends who sat with him in his silence. "We don't let our people grieve alone," his aunt told him as she set a plate of food before him. This support system reflects what Dr. Dyson calls the "communal cry"—a grief tradition rooted in the African principle of *ubuntu*: "I am because we are."

For James, healing did not come through quiet introspection but through collective remembrance. The echoes of his mother's life were everywhere—in the hymns still sung on Sundays, in the food she once cooked, now prepared by others in her honor, in the love that did not end with her passing. In African American culture, grief is not something to move past—it is something to move through, together. It is, and has always been, a team effort.

At each home and sanctuary, though shaped by different traditions, the rhythm of grief found its voice in sacred words and melodies. At the memorial for his father, David's pastor read Psalm 23, *"The Lord is my shepherd…"*. It's quiet assurance wrapping around the room like a gentle blanket. The hymn "It Is Well with My Soul" played softly, inviting tears and reflection. Across town, in Maria's candlelit living room, her family recited the Rosary and prayed the Novena, voices rising with *Padre Nuestro* and *Ave María*, while the soft strains of "Un Día a la Vez" played from her uncle's phone. Marigolds and flickering candles surrounded the ofrenda, inviting the memory of her grandmother to linger. Meanwhile, in the heart of the city, James stood in a packed sanctuary as the choir belted out "Going Up Yonder" and "I Won't Complain," hands lifted high, grief transformed into worship. The preacher thundered from John 14:1, "Let not your heart be troubled…." And saints all around him murmured prayers of strength and comfort. Whether whispered in therapy rooms, chanted in Spanish between generations, or shouted in gospel harmony from pulpit to pew, each community brought its language of healing. And in every voice, quiet or thunderous, grief was not carried alone. It was lifted by the team.

Cultural expectations shape not only how people grieve but also how they are allowed to grieve. In many White American communities, there is often an unspoken expectation to grieve privately and return to normalcy quickly, a reflection of what sociologists' call "emotional restraint" in Western culture (Neimeyer, 2014). In contrast, African American traditions encourage outward expression, with Dr. Michael Eric Dyson noting that "Black grief is loud because Black trauma is generational" (*Tears We Cannot Stop*, 2017). Hispanic families, bound by deep Catholic and indigenous influences, embrace prolonged mourning through rituals like Novenas and Día de los Muertos, reinforcing the idea that the dead remain spiritually connected to the living (Pew Research, 2021). These expectations can shape an individual's experience of loss. Someone raised in a culture that values stoicism and may feel guilty for grieving too openly, while another raised in a communal setting might struggle with silence. As Howard Thurman emphasizes that spirituals remind us that, "There is in every person an abiding need to be understood in sorrow," but whether that understanding comes through solitude, prayer circles, or a full church choir depends largely on the culture that raised them (*Deep River and The Negro Spiritual Speaks of Life and Death*). No matter the cultural lens, grief is not just personal; it is shaped by the rules, traditions, and unspoken expectations of the communities we call home.

REFERENCES

American Journal of Cultural Sociology. 2020. "Ritualizing Memory: Cultural Approaches to Mourning in Hispanic Communities." *Am J Cult Sociol*, 8(3), 221-239.

Dyson, M. E. (2017). *Tears We Cannot Stop: A Sermon to White America*—St. Martin's Press.

Neimeyer, R. A. (2014). "Meaning Reconstruction in Grief: A Commentary." *Death Studies*, 38(1-5), 61–69.

Pew Research Center. (2021). *Faith Among Hispanic Americans*. https://www.pewresearch.org

Journal of Black Studies. (2020). "Mourning in Community: The Role of African American Churches in Bereavement." *J Black Stud*, 51(1), 5-24.

Journal of Palliative Medicine. (2018). "Spiritual and Cultural Aspects of End-of-Life Care." *J Palliat Med*, 21(8), 1011-1016.

Thurman, H. (1975). *Deep River and The Negro Spiritual Speaks of Life and Death*. Friends United Press.

CHRISTIAN GRIEF,
THEN, IS NOT SILENT OR
SOLITARY.

Chapter 4:

THE COACH'S INFLUENCE – HOW RELIGION SHAPES THE GRIEVING PROCESS

In the game of basketball, a coach sets the tone—crafting a culture, laying out strategy, and guiding how the team will respond in the heat of battle. The same is true when it comes to grief. Religion, much like a seasoned coach, offers a spiritual framework that shapes how individuals process pain, find meaning in loss, and move forward with hope. Where a coach calls the plays on the court, faith offers sacred texts, rituals, and community support that help navigate the long, unpredictable season of sorrow. Grief is not a solo sport—it demands a team, a game plan, and often, a higher power whispering reminders of purpose when emotions threaten to run the floor.

Take, for example, two very different coaching philosophies: Ed Cooley, who led the Providence Friars from 2014 to 2023, built his teams on fundamentals, defense, and grit—emphasizing patience, control, and discipline. His teams weathered storms by staying grounded, trusting the process, and playing together. In contrast, Rick Pitino, known for his aggressive pressure defense and a fast-paced, three-point heavy offense, pushed his players to force the game, create chaos, and capitalize on momentum. Both strategies had their victories, but they reflect contrasting ways of facing adversity. Grief works similarly. Some approach loss like Cooley—with steady faith, structured routines, and quiet perseverance. Others, like Pitino's squads, charge into the pain, relying on bold expressions, passionate outbursts, and rapid-fire efforts to find meaning. Neither is wrong. Both require a coach. And in life, that coach is often faith.

As a hospice chaplain, I've stood at the bedside of people from many walks of faith—and from none. I've watched Jewish families gather to recite the Shema and held hands with Christians singing "Amazing Grace" through tears. I've also sat quietly beside atheists and spiritual skeptics who didn't cling to a particular tradition but still welcomed the presence of another soul in their final moments. Some held tightly to their beliefs, drawing strength from sacred words and time-honored rituals. Others drifted from the faith they once knew, unsure of what came next. But in those moments—when breaths slowed, when the room grew still— what often mattered most wasn't doctrine, but presence. Just knowing someone was there, witnessing their life and honoring their exit, seemed to offer a certain peace that words alone couldn't always give.

In the Jewish tradition, grief unfolds within a sacred rhythm, each step held by ritual and ancient wisdom. I remember talking to a Jewish neighbor who had just lost a significant relative, and he explained the space of reverence as they began *sitting shiva*, the seven-day mourning period that immediately follows burial. Visitors came not with answers, but with a quiet presence, offering comfort through shared stories and meals. "Shiva allows mourners to be enveloped by community," one rabbi shared in a continuing education seminar, "to be carried when they cannot stand on their own." It was a living example of *Pirkei Avot 1:6*: "Provide yourself with a teacher, acquire for yourself a friend, and judge every person favorably." In this case, the community itself became both teacher and friend, helping the grieving navigate the valley of loss.

Jewish mourning practices continue long after shiva, offering a framework of remembrance that sustains mourners through the months and even years ahead. The *Kaddish*, a prayer that praises God and affirms life rather than focusing on death, is recited daily for eleven months in memory of a parent. Each year on the anniversary of the death— *yahrzeit*—a candle is lit, and the name of the loved one is spoken aloud during synagogue services. These rituals keep grief from becoming an isolated burden. Instead, they weave memory into the daily fabric of life, allowing space for both pain and healing. As it is written in *Ecclesiastes Rabbah 7:1*, "The day of death is better than the day of birth," not because loss is easy, but because in honoring the dead, the living are reminded of the holiness of time and the enduring power of love. For those who practice Judaism, grief is never meant to be walked alone. It is shared, sanctified, and stretched across generations.

In the quiet moments following death, the Islamic faith provides a deeply spiritual and communal guide for grieving. I recall standing beside a Muslim family as they prepared for the *Janazah*, the Islamic funeral rite. There was no wailing or dramatic display—only purposeful movement and gentle reverence. The body of their loved one was washed, shrouded in simple white cloth, and placed facing Mecca. The *Janazah Salah*, or funeral prayer, was offered in congregation, not just by family, but by the entire faith community. "O Allah, forgive our living and our dead, those present and those absent, our young and our old, our males and our females," the imam recited. This prayer, part of the *Janazah*, wasn't only for the deceased—it was for everyone. It was as if the burden of loss was being lifted, piece by piece, by every voice that joined in. As the Prophet Muhammad (peace be upon him) said, "Visit the sick and follow the funeral processions; it will remind you of the Hereafter" (*Sahih Muslim* 977a). In Islam, grief is never detached from eternity.

What struck me most was how grief in the Islamic tradition is balanced with unwavering hope and community. Mourning isn't prolonged or made theatrical; instead, it's structured, deeply rooted in trust in God's will (*Qadr*). The family enters a three-day mourning period, during which friends and neighbors come not only to console but to pray, to share meals, and to affirm faith in Allah's mercy. *Dua* (supplications) are offered regularly, such as: "O Allah, make his grave spacious and fill it with light." These prayers are often recited not only in the days immediately after death but during *dhikr* (remembrance) gatherings for weeks and even years to come. The support doesn't fade. In Islam, grief is not simply endured—it is honored, softened through prayer, and held together by a believing community. Like a tightly run team, each person knows their role: to be present, to pray, and to believe in the mercy of the Most Compassionate.

I remember standing near the hospital bed of a woman whose time on earth was drawing to a close. Her breathing had slowed, her family gathered tightly around her, and her Bible rested open on the nightstand to 1 Thessalonians 4:16-17, "For the Lord himself will descend from heaven with a shout, with the voice of an archangel and with the trumpet of God. And the dead in Christ shall rise first…" In that room, there was no panic—only quiet anticipation, like the moment before a choir sings the final note. Her family prayed, hands clasped, asking for peace in her passing and strength in their sorrow. Their strength in sorrow reminded me of when my wise old Granddaddy, Sir T. D. Wade, Sr., died. I had already discovered that wisdom often came wrapped in wrinkled hands and slow, deliberate speech by the time I was seven. The older folks in my family said I had an "old head" on young shoulders, but I just knew I liked being around Granddaddy. He was my sage, life coach, long before the world ever gave a name to such things. He had a way of distilling life's greatest lessons into simple, unforgettable phrases. *"Every tub got to stand on its own bottom." "Don't hurry through life."* And my favorite, *"Sometimes, you just got to watch the grass grow."* He understood things most people overlooked: the way the wind whispered warnings of coming storms, how a garden could teach patience, how money moved in the world. I soaked it all in, knowing even then that his words would shape my future. When he passed at 88, I felt sad but no anguish, only gratitude. He had lived long, loved well, and left behind a legacy of quiet strength. And I was proud—proud to have sat at his feet, to have listened, to have learned.

When a believer dies, such as my grandfather, the Christian community activates like a well-coached team in the final quarter. Pastors prepare resolutions to honor the life lived—often read aloud during the service with stirring declarations: "Whereas, our dearly beloved has fought a good fight… therefore be it resolved…" Deacons and church mothers gather to coordinate food, ushering meals into the grieving home with love wrapped in foil pans and Tupperware. Prayer chains ignite, scripture is shared, and handwritten cards flow like water. The *repast,* that sacred fellowship meal after the funeral, becomes a continuation of worship, stories told between bites, laughter braided with tears. As Dr. Renita Weems reminds us, "Our faith teaches us to lament, to grieve in rhythm with hope." The Black church doesn't just bury its dead. It lifts them, celebrates their legacy, and reminds the living that death has no sting when Christ is the victory. For Christians, especially in the Black church tradition, death is not the end of the story. It is the doorway to resurrection, the moment when faith meets fulfillment, and the promise of eternal life begins. As Dr. James Cone, the father of Black Liberation Theology, once wrote, "The Christian gospel is more than a transcendent reality; it is a liberating word for the oppressed, promising new life beyond the suffering of this world."

At funerals, the Christian doctrine of the resurrection takes center stage. The preacher's voice rises with assurance, echoing Paul's triumphant cry from 1 Corinthians 15:55 "O death, where is thy sting? O grave, where is thy victory?" This hope of resurrection isn't abstract. It's tangible, lived, and preached and clung to in times of loss. It is the theological glue that holds grieving hearts together. Bishop T.D. Jakes once said, "Faith doesn't always take you out of the problem, but it takes you through the problem." For many Black Christians, grief is carried through worship— through music, prayer, and the rock-solid belief that one day, they will see their loved ones again when that great trumpet sounds.

Christian grief, then, is not silent or solitary. It's played in choirs and congregations, preached from pulpits, and comforted through casseroles. It is the collective groan and shout of a people who believe that joy comes in the morning, and that God will wipe every tear from their eyes. In death, as in life, they rely on one another and on a Savior who promised to return.

REFERENCE LIST

Cone, J. H. (2011). *The Cross and the Lynching Tree*. Orbis Books.

Holy Bible, New King James Version. (1982). Thomas Nelson. (1 Thessalonians 4:16–17; 1 Corinthians 15:55)

Jakes, T. D. (2006). *Reposition Yourself: Living Life Without Limits*. Atria Books.

Muslim, I. (n.d.). *Sahih Muslim*, 977a. Retrieved from https://sunnah.com/muslim:977a

Pirkei Avot 1:6. (n.d.). *Ethics of the Fathers*. Retrieved from https://www.sefaria.org/Pirkei_Avot.1.6

Weems, R. J. (1999). *Listening for God: A Minister's Journey through Silence and Doubt*. Simon & Schuster.

Ecclesiastes Rabbah 7:1. (n.d.). *Midrash Rabbah*. Retrieved from https://www.sefaria.org/Ecclesiastes_Rabbah.7.1

Chapter 5:

THE EMOTIONAL ROSTER – THE MANY FACES OF GRIEF

The sun hung low in the sky, casting long shadows over the freshly chalked baselines. I was ten years old, standing on the edge of the dugout in my crisp blue jersey, my heart pounding with a mix of excitement and nerves. This was my first season of Little League baseball, and I was officially a Royal. The moment I slipped on that uniform, something clicked. I wasn't just playing for the Optimist Club team; I had found my Major League heroes. From that day on, the Kansas City Royals became my team, and their fearless leader, George Brett, became my favorite player. A thirteen-time All-Star, Brett played with grit, passion, and an unshakable determination, and I wanted to play the game the same way. But as I took my place on the field, gripping my glove with sweaty hands, I quickly realized something: baseball wasn't just about my performance. It was about the team—nine players, each with a different job, working together toward one goal.

Grief, I would later learn, operates in much the same way. Like a baseball team, grief has different players, emotions that show up in their own time, each with a distinct role. Shock stands on the pitcher's mound, throwing fastballs of disbelief. Anger crouches behind home plate, ready to argue every call. Sadness roams the outfield, covering more ground than expected, while hope waits on the bench, uncertain but prepared to step in when needed. Just as a team can't win with only one great player, grief isn't processed through just one emotion. It takes all of them, working together, sometimes in chaos, sometimes in harmony, to carry us through the game of loss. At ten years old, I only knew baseball, but

33

years later, I came to understand that grief, like the sport I loved, is never faced alone.

The first time I stepped onto that baseball field at age ten, I didn't know what to expect. I had practiced in the backyard, thrown balls against the garage door, and watched endless games on TV, but the reality of being in the game was different. I wanted to do everything right—catch every ball, make every play—but baseball, like life, doesn't work that way. There were bad hops, errors, and strikeouts. And just as I had to adjust to the unpredictable nature of the game, I would one day have to adjust to the unpredictable waves of grief. When I lost my brother, Ernest, I found myself facing a team I had never wanted to play against—the emotions of loss. Each one took its place on the field, some staying longer than others, but all playing their role in the grieving process.

Denial was the first to step onto the mound, throwing fastballs I wasn't ready to face. This can't be happening. Not to him. Not to our family. Elisabeth Kübler-Ross, the renowned psychiatrist who pioneered the five stages of grief, described denial as the mind's way of cushioning the blow: "Denial helps us to pace our feelings of grief. There is a grace in denial. It is nature's way of letting in only as much as we can handle." At first, I went through the motions, convinced there had been a mistake, that I would wake up and things would be different. Like a batter refusing to swing, I stood frozen, unwilling to face the reality that my brother was really gone. But grief doesn't allow you to stay in one place for long.

Soon, Anger took its position behind home plate, ready to challenge every call. I accepted the call to a fulltime pastorate in Yazoo City, Mississippi. This meant that I would have to commute from Yazoo City to Murfreesboro, Tennessee since my wife worked there and our children were in school and preschool there. Making the long drive week after week and unsure of what lay ahead was daunting. But God had already placed a family in my path—the Strongs. Charlie, Mary Ann, and their youngest daughter, Cynthia, welcomed me into their home, offering me a place to stay in what they called the "prophet's quarters." They fed me, laughed with me, prayed with me, and made a strange place feel like home. Mary Ann, with her warm spirit, made sure I had my fill of black-eyed peas with okra, and over time, I came to love that dish and my new family as my own. So, when I moved to pastor in a different city, I got word that the queen of my new family was sick. The illness progressed and gripped Mary Ann, stealing her strength and dimming her once-bright light. I prayed fervently. But prayers didn't stop the inevitable. She worsened, and then, she was gone. I was heartbroken. And I was angry. Why her, God? Why, sweet Mary Ann? The woman who had shown me kindness when I was a stranger, the one who had set a place for me at her table—why did she have to die?

I was angry at God for allowing this to happen to her. Even more so, I was mad at Ernest himself for leaving us so soon. Anger in grief isn't neat. It flares up unexpectedly, sometimes directed at those we love most, sometimes turned inward. David Kessler explained, "Anger is pain's bodyguard." It shields us, gives us something to fight against when the reality of loss feels too unbearable. Just like a frustrated catcher arguing with the umpire, I wanted to protest every unfair moment. But no matter how loud I got, I couldn't change the call that had already been made. My anger was chased away upon being asked to eulogize my black-eyed peas and okra coinsurer and friend.

Then came Bargaining, pacing in the dugout, whispering, *If only I had called him more. If only we had caught the illness sooner. If only I had prayed harder.* Bargaining is the illusion of control, the desperate attempt to rewrite the past in hopes of changing the present. It has been described as the "what if" stage, where our minds race to find a way out of the pain. I replayed moments in my head, searching for the one decision that might have led to a different outcome. Grief is never just about losing someone; it's about learning to live with the empty spaces they leave behind.

He was my friend for over 40 years—first a mentor, then a colleague, and finally, one of my own church members when I became his pastor in June 2023. Our bond started in my teenage years over sports, strengthened through ministry, and deepened through shared life experiences. Even with his illness, he showed up—helping us find a home, picking up a paintbrush, offering his support in ways I didn't fully appreciate until he was gone. He passed away on a Friday night, right after prayer with his wife, leaving behind the weight of unspoken gratitude and lingering questions. Should I have let him help with the house, knowing he wasn't well? Why didn't I say no when he could have been resting between doctors' visits. These thoughts have crossed my mind from time to time in the immediate aftermath. Months have passed now since I stood and preached my mentor's eulogy while wiping a few tears, and since we laid him to rest. However, quiet grief-like moments have been known to appear while driving past the exit to his house, in conversations with his wife, in flashes of memory that reminded me of his wisdom and kindness. Yet, in walking with his family through their loss, I found healing too. Helping them forge a new path forward has reminded me that even in loss, love continues its work, it supports, it strengthens, and it carries us through. But just like in baseball, you can't go back and replay an inning. The game moves forward whether you're ready or not.

Depression took its place in the outfield in the immediate aftermath of Ernie's death, covering more ground than I ever thought possible. Unlike anger, which feels like movement, depression settles in like fog, making everything heavier. I didn't want to get out of bed to see my hospice patients. I didn't want to talk. The world kept moving, but I felt stuck, left behind. Kessler described this stage not as a sign of mental illness but as "a very appropriate response to a great loss." The truth is, grief changes you. It forces you to carry something you never asked for. And in those moments of deep sorrow, it feels impossible to believe that joy will ever return.

Grieving alone can feel like a desperate base runner caught in a rundown between second and third—darting back and forth, trying to outmaneuver the inevitable tag, but slowly realizing that escape is unlikely without help. It's a painful metaphor, yet one that captures the exhausting emotional limbo many people experience when trying to navigate loss without a team. While some sprint forward, trying to outrun sorrow, others retreat to familiar ground, only to be forced back again by waves of pain, confusion, and unanswered questions. This constant emotional back-and-forth drains the spirit and clouds the mind, often leaving individuals more isolated than before. Many choose to grieve alone because of internalized beliefs that vulnerability equals weakness, or because they've learned—often from childhood or traumatic past experiences—that expressing pain is not safe. According to clinical psychologist Dr. Robert Neimeyer, "Bereavement isolates us not only from the one we love, but also from the community around us, unless we are willing to reach out and let others in" (Neimeyer, *Techniques of Grief Therapy*, 2012). Sadly, not everyone knows how to reach out, and some don't believe they'll be received if they do. Cultural expectations, especially among men or in certain communities, also play a role, pushing people to "be strong" or "move on" prematurely, which often backfires. "Studies show that while support is a vital buffer against complicated grief, those without a social network or those who feel ashamed of their emotions are at much higher risk for prolonged suffering and depression symptoms (Stroebe & Schut, 2001; Stroebe et al., 2006; Lee et al., 2020)." Grieving alone may feel like an act of bravery, but more often, it's a survival instinct gone awry—a lonely run-down that ends not in safety, but in emotional and spiritual burnout.

But then, slowly, Acceptance stepped up to bat. Not as a victory, not as an end to grief, but as a willingness to keep playing. Kübler-Ross wrote, "Acceptance is not about liking the loss. It is about acknowledging all that has been lost and learning to live with that loss." Acceptance doesn't mean you stop grieving. It doesn't mean the pain disappears. It simply means you find a way to carry it differently. Over time, I learned that grief, like baseball, is a team sport. No one emotion carries the entire game. Each has its role, and each must be acknowledged. And just like stepping onto that field at ten years old, I had to trust the process, knowing that even in the hardest moments, I wasn't alone.

Grief doesn't just sit quietly in the background; it plays out in real time, influencing how we think, speak, and act, often in ways we don't fully recognize. One moment, I was the composed team captain, holding it together for everyone else, and the next, I was slamming doors in frustration, snapping at people who were only trying to help. Anger made me restless, pacing the house at odd hours, while depression drained me, making even the simplest tasks feel impossible. Psychologists note that these shifting behaviors are part of the body's attempt to process loss. It is explained that grief is not linear; emotions come and go like waves, sometimes pulling us under before letting us surface again. "We don't move on from grief," Kessler writes. "We move forward with it." Looking back, I can see how each emotion took its turn, affecting not only how I felt but also how I interacted with the world, sometimes shutting people out, sometimes clinging to them, always searching for a way to make sense of a reality I never wanted.

In a similar way, the faces of grief and loss can be seen on one of the stars of Good Times, my favorite TV show of the 1970s. Every night of its weekly airing, I sat in front of the screen, humming along to the theme song…

"Good Times!Anytime you need a payment!
Good Times!
Anytime you need a friend!
Good Times!
Anytime you're out from under!
Not getting hassled, not getting hustled!
Keeping your head above water,
Making a wave when you can…

Temporary layoffs (Good Times!)
Easy credit rip-offs (Good Times!)
Scratching and surviving (Good Times!)
Hanging in a chow line (Good Times!)
Ain't we lucky we got 'em?
Good Times!"

I was right there in the Evans' apartment, laughing at J.J.'s jokes, looking at Thelma's beauty, lauding Michael's smarts, longing to have James's muscles, learning from Florida's wisdom, and rooting for them to make it through. An iconic scene offers a powerful example of grief's raw intensity. When Florida Evans (played by Esther Rolle) learned of her husband James' death, she did not cry at the funeral, she appears to join in celebrative storytelling about James at the repast in their apartment at first, only after the guests have gone to suddenly explode in rage, smashing the punch bowl and shouting, "Damn, Damn, Damn!" This moment became etched into cultural memory because it so vividly captured the unpredictable and overwhelming nature of grief. Florida's emotional eruption aligns with what psychologists identify as the various "faces" of grief — anger, denial, sadness, guilt, and acceptance.

The powerful *Good Times* scene of Florida Evans' emotional eruption highlights the multifaceted nature of grief. Whether manifesting as anger, denial, sadness, or guilt, each "face" of grief reveals the complexity of the mourning process. By exploring these emotional responses, we gain a deeper understanding of grief's unpredictable yet necessary journey. Just as Florida's grief found expression in both rage and tears, so too bereaved individuals must be allowed to experience the full range of emotions that accompany loss. Healing, in time, comes not by suppressing these faces of grief but by embracing them as part of the path toward acceptance and renewed strength.

Recognizing grief-related emotions is one of the hardest parts of the journey because they rarely show up in a way that's easy to identify. When I lost my brother, I expected sadness, maybe even anger, but what I didn't expect was exhaustion, the brain fog, the way little things suddenly became overwhelming. Some days, I felt fine, like I had made peace with everything, only to find myself feeling down at the sight of his handwriting on an old birthday card. Grief doesn't follow a schedule, and it doesn't always announce itself in obvious ways. Proverbs 14:13 says, "Even in laughter the heart may ache, and rejoicing may end in grief." That was my reality—smiling on the outside while carrying a deep, invisible weight. Experts explain that grief can manifest as forgetfulness, irritability, loss of appetite, or even physical pain. David Kessler notes that "grief must be witnessed," meaning we must acknowledge what we're feeling rather than suppressing it. But that's easier said than done. Most of us were never taught how to grieve. We were taught to be strong, to push forward to "trust God and move on." Yet Ecclesiastes 3:4 reminds us that there is "a time to weep and a time to laugh, a time to mourn and a time to dance." If we don't give ourselves permission to recognize our pain, we risk carrying it in unhealthy ways—through anger that never subsides, isolation that deepens, or even bitterness that hardens our hearts.

Moving through grief is not about rushing to the end but about learning how to walk with it, step by step. Jesus Himself understood the weight of sorrow, as seen in John 11:35, where it simply says, "Jesus wept." He didn't dismiss the pain of loss, even knowing He would raise Lazarus from the dead. Instead, He grieved. That tells me grief is not weakness. What a profound thought. It is not a lack of faith. It is love in its raw and aching form. So, how do we proceed through it? First, by allowing ourselves to feel without shame. Journaling, talking to a trusted friend, or even speaking aloud to God about the pain can help. Second, seek support. Just as a baseball team relies on each player, we need people who can help us process what we're feeling. And third, by holding on to hope, even when it feels distant. As Psalm 34:18 reminds us, "The Lord is close to the brokenhearted and saves those who are crushed in spirit." Grief is not a straight path, but a winding road with setbacks and moments of unexpected peace. Healing doesn't mean forgetting; it means learning to live again, carrying love forward in a new way.

REFERENCE LIST

Kessler, D. (2019). *Finding meaning: The sixth stage of grief.* Scribner.

Kessler, D., & Kübler-Ross, E. (2005). *On grief and grieving: Finding the meaning of grief through the five stages of loss.* Scribner.

Kübler-Ross, E. (1969). *On death and dying.* Macmillan.

Neimeyer, R. A. (2012). *Techniques of grief therapy: Creative practices for counseling the bereaved.* Routledge.

Stroebe, M., & Schut, H. (2001). Risk factors in bereavement outcome: A conceptual framework. In M. Stroebe, R. O. Hansson, W. Stroebe, & H. Schut (Eds.), Handbook of bereavement research: Consequences, coping, and care (pp. 349–371). Washington, DC: American Psychological Association.

Stroebe, M., Folkman, S., Hansson, R. O., & Schut, H. (2006). The prediction of bereavement outcome: Development of an integrative risk factor framework. Social Science & Medicine, 63(9), 2440–2451.

Lee, S. A., Neimeyer, R. A., & Chow, A. Y. (2020). Guilt and shame as predictors of complicated grief and depression in bereaved adults. OMEGA—Journal of Death and Dying, 82(1), 128–147.

Chapter 6:

THE INJURY REPORT – THE PHYSICAL TOLL OF GRIEF

Kobe Bryant's basketball career was a masterclass in relentless determination, an unyielding pursuit of greatness fueled by a fire that never seemed to flicker. From his teenage years straight out of high school to his final farewell in a 60-point blaze of glory, Kobe's legacy was etched not only in stats and rings but in grit. His body absorbed the grind of seventeen seasons before it betrayed him one unforgettable night in April 2013. The Los Angeles Lakers were locked in a playoff push when Kobe drove past Harrison Barnes, planted his left foot, and crumpled to the floor. He had torn his Achilles tendon—one of the most dreaded injuries in sports. Most players would have been carried off. Kobe stood up, walked to the free-throw line, and knocked down two shots with a leg that had just snapped. It wasn't just heroic; it was painful, spiritual, and surreal. It was Kobe.

But that moment of collapse wasn't just about the physical break. It cracked open the man behind the legend. The rehab was brutal. Hours of isolated stretching, pain, and surgical soreness. Yet Kobe wasn't alone. Behind the scenes stood a team of healers, believers, and steady hands: Gary Vitti, the Lakers' head athletic trainer who had been with him from the beginning; Dr. Neal ElAttrache, who performed the surgery; and his wife, Vanessa, whose quiet strength helped steady his storm. Kobe leaned on their expertise, their encouragement, and their honesty. Each step, from walking again to dribbling, became a shared victory. His comeback wasn't just a testament to willpower; it was a portrait of grief, grief for lost ability, for the fear of a fading legacy, and how, with a team around you, even the most legendary warrior learns how to heal.

Just like athletes rebuilding their bodies after injury, those grieving must tend to the wounds that cannot be seen but are just as real. When a player goes down—whether it's a torn ligament, fractured bone, or ruptured tendon—the first step isn't heroic. It's humble. It's rest. It's admitting something is broken. Trainers wrap ice around swelling, doctors order MRIs, and coaches shuffle lineups, all while the athlete wrestles with the ache of absence. They aren't running plays; they're learning to walk again. They aren't chasing victory; they're clinging to stability. Grief is no different. When loss hits, it knocks the wind out of you and breaks you in places you didn't know could break. And yet, we often try to power through, numb the pain, or mask it with busyness. But healing demands more. Just like an athlete must eat, sleep, stretch, and slowly rebuild strength, those grieving must care for their physical bodies in ways that feel almost impossible—drinking water when their throat is tight with sorrow, walking outside when the weight of grief begs them to lie down, breathing deeply even when the air feels thin. There are no shortcuts. The body holds the sorrow. And like the injured star surrounded by a team of experts, grievers also need a circle of friends who bring soup, ears who listen without fixing, and pastors who sit without preaching. Every ache, every tear, every hour of sleep becomes part of the rehab. And one day, maybe not today, they rise, still hurting, still healing—but stronger than they ever imagined.

When Ernest died, it was as if the world stopped turning for a span. But my body kept moving, and not in the way I'd hoped. It stumbled. It groaned. It forgot how to rest. In those early days, I wasn't just emotionally drained; I was physically exhausted. Life kept coming. The pastorate, chaplain visits continued to amass. Grief doesn't politely confine itself to the heart. It invades the body like a thief in the night, robbing you of energy, disrupting sleep, and dulling your senses. I'd wake up tired and go to bed more tired, as if mourning had replaced rest with a permanent fog. What I didn't know then, but have come to learn, is that this kind of fatigue is one of the most common and overlooked ways grief manifests in the body. According to the *American Psychological Association*, "The stress of grief can take a toll on the body, causing fatigue and lowering the immune response."

Medical studies confirm what grievers often discover the hard way: grief can lead to tension headaches like unwanted houseguests settle in and take more than a nap or drink of water to shake off. Migraines and even gastrointestinal distress can show up. The stress hormone cortisol surges in the body, especially when sorrow is suppressed or ignored, weakening the immune system and leaving us vulnerable to colds, infections, and longer recovery times. One doctor described it this way: "Your body hears everything your heart doesn't say."

But it wasn't just the physical symptoms that worried me. Mentally, I began to unravel. Focus became slippery. Conversations felt like mazes. I was forgetful, irritable, sometimes numb. Grief can mimic depression and often does. The National Institute of Mental Health reports that grief and depression share symptoms like sadness, loss of interest, and trouble sleeping, but grief, when prolonged or complicated, can become clinical depression if not addressed. I didn't want to talk about it at first, especially as a man taught to be strong, to 'push through.' But grief isn't a mountain you conquer; it's a storm that you weather and storms require shelter. Sometimes that shelter is a therapist's office, a quiet walk with a friend, or simply permission to feel what you feel without shame.

There is no shortcut through this terrain, but there are practical steps. Hydration, even when water tastes like nothing. Movement, even if it's just a five-minute walk. Sleep hygiene, like turning off screens an hour before bed or creating a peaceful nighttime routine. Journaling the swirl of thoughts and emotions. And perhaps most importantly, reaching out—to a pastor, a counselor, a grief support group, or someone who's walked the road before. Healing doesn't happen in isolation. Just as an athlete needs a medical team, grieving hearts need a circle of care. We are not meant to do this alone.

So, if you find yourself in the middle of grief, and your body feels like it's giving up on you—pause. Breathe. Know that what you're feeling isn't weakness. It's human. It's part of the cost of love. But also know this: with the right support, your body and your soul can begin to heal. The team you gather, whether professional, spiritual, or personal, can help you lift what you were never meant to carry alone. Because grief is a team sport. And the road back to yourself is one walked best with others by your side.

When Kobe Bryant tore his Achilles in 2013, the injury wasn't just to his body; it was to his identity. For a man who lived to compete, who defined himself by his work ethic and will to win, the rupture was more than physical. It was psychological. "The mind is the most powerful thing we have," Kobe once said. "You can always control your effort and your focus." That mindset, what the world came to know as the *Mamba Mentality*, wasn't just bravado. It was survival. He understood that recovery began in the mind before it ever showed up in the body. Doctors repaired the tendon, trainers supervised rehab, but it was Kobe's belief in his future, his refusal to let pain have the final word, that pulled him through. Research from Harvard Medical School confirms what he lived: "Mental health and physical health are fundamentally linked. People living with chronic stress, depression, or anxiety often experience physical symptoms like muscle tension, fatigue, and a suppressed immune system." Grief works the same way. It clouds judgment, increases cortisol, slows healing, and can literally weigh the body down. In my own journey through loss, I discovered that if I didn't fight for my mind, I'd lose my body too. Days spent in emotional despair translated into sleepless nights, tension headaches, and chest tightness. But like Kobe, I had to talk to myself louder than my grief talked to me. I had to summon my own version of the Mamba Mentality, not to "power through," but to be mentally tough enough to rest when needed, to cry without shame, and to believe that healing was possible even when it felt distant. Mental toughness in grief isn't about pretending you're okay; it's about showing up for yourself and letting others show up too. It's choosing to engage in the hard work of healing, even when you're exhausted. Just like Kobe didn't rehab alone, neither should the grieving. Because whether you're getting back on the court or back to life, the right mindset and the right team make all the difference.

When my brother Ernest passed, I remember waking up in the middle of the night with tightness in my chest—not panic, but something deeper, heavier. It felt like my heart was doing its own grieving, pounding against the weight of a world that no longer had him in it. What I didn't realize at the time was that this wasn't just emotion. It was biology. Grief affects the heart in literal, measurable ways. There's even a name for it: *broken heart syndrome*, or stress cardiomyopathy. According to the American Heart Association, "Broken heart syndrome can be brought on by

44

sudden emotional stress, such as the death of a loved one, and it can lead to severe, short-term heart muscle failure." The symptoms often mimic a heart attack, shortness of breath, chest pain, irregular heartbeat, and they can be just as dangerous. Dr. Ilan Wittstein of Johns Hopkins, one of the leading researchers on the syndrome, notes, "The heart is physically affected by grief. Stress hormones weaken the heart muscle, disrupting its ability to pump blood effectively." For me trips to my primary care physician and cardiologist resulted in good reports, even the stress test was in normal range.

What's startling is how quickly grief can compromise heart health, especially when it's ignored or pushed aside. A study published in *Circulation* found that the risk of heart attack is 21 times higher within the first 24 hours after the death of a loved one and remains elevated for several weeks (Mostofsky et al., 2012). That's not just poetic language. It's a medical reality. Dr. Kathy Shear, a psychiatrist and grief expert from Columbia University, describes grief as a full-body experience, and research confirms it commonly affects your sleep, your appetite, and your cardiovascular system." And when we grieve in isolation, when we try to carry the pain alone, the heart bears an even greater burden. I've seen it myself and in others: the widower who stopped eating, the mother who couldn't sleep, the friend who never laughed the same way again. This is why community matters, not just emotionally, but physiologically. When others walk with you through sorrow, when you cry with someone beside you, it's not just your spirit that's lifted. It's your heart, too. Grief is a weight too heavy to carry alone, and sometimes, your literal life depends on someone else helping you hold it.

When an elite athlete goes down with an injury, the path to recovery doesn't begin with hustle—it begins with stillness. Ice, elevation, rest, nutrition, sleep. Self-care is not a luxury for the injured; it's the plan. Yet when we grieve, especially in a culture that prizes toughness and productivity, we often forget that we, too, are healing from something life-altering. We try to "stay strong," keep moving, check the boxes. But as I learned after losing my brother, healing requires a conscious commitment to caring for both body and mind. The National Institute on Aging states that grief can cause "changes in sleep patterns, appetite, and energy," and that "self-care practices like regular meals, light exercise, and rest can significantly improve coping capacity" (*NIA, 2020*). What athletes do for swollen joints and torn muscles, grievers must do for wounded hearts. The sooner we accept that, the sooner the healing can begin.

Miss Alberta after her husband passed. She wore quiet strength like a crown, dawning her silver hair. She said something I'll never forget: "Baby, you got to be kind to yourself when the world ain't. If you don't water the garden of your soul, it'll dry up." What wonderful words of wisdom. Echoed in scientific literature. Studies from the American Psychological Association show that people who actively engage in self-care during grief—simple things like walking, journaling, or connecting with nature—report lower levels of depression and anxiety over time.-She understood that healing doesn't roar; sometimes, it whispers.

Even Scripture invites us into a balanced, whole-person recovery. Proverbs 17:22 says, "A cheerful heart is good medicine, but a crushed spirit dries up the bones." That's not a denial of grief—it's a call to protect the spirit while the body recovers. Romans 12:4-5 reminds us, "For just as each of us has one body with many members… so in Christ we, though many, form one body, and each member belongs to all the others." The same way a strained hamstring relies on the rest of the body to compensate, a grieving soul needs the support of others to make it through. Self-care, then, is not selfish, it's sacred. It is the quiet agreement between your body and your spirit that you are worth saving, day by day. And it becomes even more powerful when practiced in the community, when others remind you to eat, rest, breathe, and believe. Because whether you're on the road to a comeback or climbing out of sorrow, no one heals alone. Getting through grief takes more than inner strength. It takes a circle of care.

In the end, self-care isn't about escaping grief. It's about equipping yourself to survive it. It's the intentional, sacred act of saying, "I matter, even in my pain." Whether you're mourning a loss or mending a torn ligament, the journey requires gentleness, structure, and support. As Pastor Howard-John Wesley once said, "Rest is not a reward for finishing the work—it's God's command so you can keep going." Iyanla Vanzant reminds us, "Self-care is not selfish. You cannot serve from an empty vessel." From the sports world, Serena Williams said it simply: "I've learned to listen to my body and give myself grace. Healing takes time." And licensed therapist Nedra Glover Tawwab offers this wisdom: "Self-care is how you take your power back." Grief will try to drain you. Life will push you to neglect yourself. But self-care is the quiet rebellion that says, "I will heal, and I don't have to do it alone." It's the team sport you play with your spirit, your body, your people—and God.

REFERENCE LIST

American Heart Association. (2022). *Broken heart syndrome: What's going on?* https://www.heart.org

Harvard Medical School. (2021). *The link between mental health and physical health.* https://www.health.harvard.edu

Mostofsky, E., Maclure, M., Sherwood, J.B., & Mittleman, M.A. (2012). *Risk of acute myocardial infarction after the death of a significant person in one's life: The case-crossover study. Circulation,* 125(3), 491–496.

National Institute on Aging. (2020). *Grief: Coping with the loss of a loved one.* https://www.nia.nih.gov

American Psychological Association. (2020). *Grief and self-care: Psychological science insights.* https://www.apa.org

GRIEF IS A COLLECTIVE
JOURNEY, BUT THE MOST
CRUCIAL PLAYER IS THE
INNER VOICE.

Chapter 7:

LOCKER ROOM TALK - POWER OF WORD IN GRIEF

The voices we hear, both our own and those of others, shape how we navigate grief. Like a coach rallying his team before an impossible game, the words spoken into our lives can fuel resilience or deepen despair. In the 1980 Winter Olympics, Coach Herb Brooks stood before a group of young men who had been told they didn't stand a chance. The Soviet team was stronger, faster, more experienced. But Brooks refused to let his players believe they were already defeated. "Great moments are born from great opportunity," he told them. "If we played them ten times, they might win nine. But not this game. Not tonight." His words reframed the battle ahead, shifting their mindset from inevitability to possibility. In grief, the voices we listen to—our own internal dialogue and the words of those around us—can either tell us that sorrow will win every time or that, on this day, in this moment, healing is possible.

When grief hits, words become more than just sounds. They shape the way we endure, recover, and move forward. Like a team stepping onto the ice, the grieving doesn't walk alone; they are surrounded by voices. Some that lift them up and others that weigh them down. A well-placed word can be the assist that keeps someone in the game, while a careless comment can knock them off balance. The difference between the two is often a matter of awareness, intention, and timing.

Consider a grieving mother who has just lost her son. In the rawness of her sorrow, she is met with two very different responses. One friend takes her hands, looks her in the eyes, and says, "I don't have the words, but I'm here. You're not alone." Those words become a lifeline, reinforcing that she has a team around her, that even in loss, she is not abandoned. Another person, meaning well but speaking without thought, sighs and says, "At least you still have your daughter." The words land like a check against the boards, harsh, dismissive, minimizing her pain. Instead of comfort, she feels isolated, as if her grief should be measured and compared rather than honored.

Psychologist Brené Brown reminds us, "Rarely can a response make something better. What makes something better is connection." Words that help in grief don't have to fix or explain; they simply need to stand with the person in their pain. Saying, "This must be so hard, and I'm here," or even a simple, "I love you, and I'm holding space for you," acknowledges the weight of grief without trying to rush it away. In contrast, words like "You need to move on" or "Everything happens for a reason" may be meant to encourage but often make the grieving feel misunderstood or pressured to speed through their sorrow.

Grief is a team sport, and in any team dynamic, communication matters. Just as a coach's words can rally a team or break its spirit, the words spoken to the grieving can either reinforce their strength or deepen their isolation. The challenge is not in having the perfect words but in choosing to speak with compassion, to remind the grieving that they don't have to face their loss all by their lonesome.

The hardest battles in grief are often the ones fought in silence. Long after the condolences fade and the world moves on, the grieving are left to their own thoughts. What we tell ourselves in these moments can determine whether we stand back up or stay down. Like an athlete facing defeat, our internal dialogue can either push us forward or keep us on the sidelines. Dr. Myles Munroe once said, "The greatest tragedy in life is not death, but a life without purpose." In grief, purpose can feel lost, but the way we speak to ourselves can remind us that even in loss, life still calls us forward.

Take a father who has lost his wife. The house is quieter now, the routines feel hollow, and the voice in his head whispers, you'll never be whole again. You'll always be broken. That voice is the opponent, the one that wants him to believe the game is already lost. But if he shifts his inner dialogue, he can change the course of his healing. Instead of seeing himself as defeated, he tells himself, this pain is real, but I am not alone. My children still need me. I can take one step today. That single shift in perspective becomes his first step back into the game.

Motivational speaker Eric Thomas, known for his passionate encouragement, teaches, "You cannot afford to live in potential for the rest of your life. At some point, you have to unleash that potential and make something happen". Grief tempts us to stay in a cycle of what could have been, regrets, missed opportunities, and the longing for more time. But if we tell ourselves that loss is not the end of our purpose, we begin to reclaim our power. A widow who once thought, "I don't know how to go on without him, *begins to say,* He would want me to live. I can honor his life by continuing to live mine. That internal shift doesn't erase the pain, but it gives her the strength to keep moving.

Grief is a collective journey, but the most crucial player is the inner voice. What we tell ourselves in the darkest moments can be the difference between staying stuck and finding a way forward. The mind, like any muscle, needs training. When we choose to speak life to ourselves, we ignite the words of Lisa Nichols encourages, "Your story is not meant to be your fortress, your story is meant to be your fuel", to remind ourselves that we still have purpose, we begin to heal. And healing, like any great comeback, starts with a single decision—to believe that the game is not over yet.

The words spoken to the grieving can either be a warm embrace or a weight that sinks them deeper into sorrow. Just as in sports, where a coach's encouragement can turn a struggling team into champions, the right words can help a grieving heart take another step forward. But the wrong words—no matter how well-intended—can cause more harm than good. Proverbs 18:21 (NKJV) reminds us, "Death and life are in the power of the tongue, and those who love it will eat its fruit." The grieving doesn't just hear words; they feel them.

Imagine two people approaching a grieving husband at his wife's funeral. The first person places a hand on his shoulder and says, "I know it hurts. You don't have to be strong for anyone right now. Take your time." Those words acknowledge his pain and give him permission to grieve. "At least she's in a better place. God needed another angel", whispers another in bold confidence. Though meant to comfort, the phrase dismisses his sorrow, making him feel like he should be grateful instead of heartbroken. Ecclesiastes 3:4 (NKJV) reminds us there is "a time to weep, and a time to laugh; a time to mourn, and a time to dance." Grieving people don't need quick fixes; they need space to mourn.

A single mother grieving the loss of her child hears two different responses from those around her. One friend sits beside her in silence before saying, "I can't imagine your pain, but I love you, and I'm here." That statement doesn't try to explain her loss; it simply reassures her that she is not alone. Another older person, uncomfortable with her tears, offers, "Everything happens for a reason." Those words land heavily, making her feel as if she must accept her loss as part of some greater plan rather than allowing herself to grieve fully. In contrast, Jesus himself demonstrated the power of presence when he wept at Lazarus' tomb, even though he knew he would raise him John 11:35 (NKJV). Jesus, the Master Teacher and Practitioner, demonstrated the "ministry of presence" long before I learned it as a chaplain. As Henri Nouwen wrote, "When we honestly ask ourselves which person in our lives means the most to us, we often find that it is those who, instead of giving advice, have chosen rather to share our pain and touch our wounds with a warm and tender hand." (Nouwen, 1974). Sometimes, the best comfort is not in explanation, but in companionship.

Grief is a team sport, and the words we offer are either a teammate's hand lifting someone up or an unnecessary shove that knocks them down. Comforting words do not have to be profound. They simply need to be sincere. Saying, "I'm praying for you," *or* "I don't have the right words, but I'm here," can make all the difference. As Isaiah 41:10 (NKJV) assures, "Fear not, for I am with you; be not dismayed, for I am your God. I will strengthen you, yes, I will help you, I will uphold you with My righteous right hand." The grieving do not need clichés; they need truth, love, and the steady presence of those willing to walk beside them through the storm.

REFERENCES

Brown, B. (2015). Daring Greatly: How the courage to be vulnerable transforms the way we live, love, parent, and lead. Avery.

Holy Bible, New King James Version. (1982). Thomas Nelson.

Munroe, M. (2002). *Understanding your potential: Discovering the hidden you*. Destiny Image.

Nouwen, H. J. M. (1974). *Out of solitude: Three meditations on the Christian life*. Ave Maria Press.

Thomas, E. (2013). *The secret to success*. Eric Thomas & Associates.

JUST AS NO PLAYER CAN WIN A
GAME SINGLE-HANDEDLY, NO
ONE SHOULD BE EXPECTED TO
OVERCOME GRIEF WITHOUT
SUPPORT.

Chapter 8:

OVERTIME – WHEN GRIEF LINGERS LONGER THAN EXPECTED

The final seconds were slipping away, and Kentucky seemed poised to claim victory. But then, with the weight of the moment pressing down, Grant Hill launched a perfect full-court pass, and Christian Laettner, calm in the chaos, rose above the defense to sink a turnaround jumper that defied belief. Duke had won in overtime—when the game took longer than expected. Grief can feel the same way. Just when we think we're nearing the end, another wave comes, another moment stretches beyond what we imagined. Some journeys take longer than others, and like that unforgettable night in 1992, resilience, support, and the people who pass us hope when we feel we've lost control make all the difference. Grief, like basketball, is never just about one person; it's a team sport.

Basketball taught me that grief and recovery are not solo efforts. They are a team sport. In my senior year of high school, our team was unstoppable, riding a perfect 29-0 record into the state tournament. But in a heartbreaking moment, I fouled out of the game—the only time all season—with 2:53 left on the clock. Helpless on the bench, I watched as the final seconds unfolded, hope rising and crashing with every possession. Our last shot was a clean, open look, bounced off the rim, and a teammate tipped it in just as the buzzer sounded. For a fleeting moment, we thought we had won. But then, the referee's wave cut through the air like a dagger—*No good.* We lost. Just like that, our perfect season was over. I was crushed. I didn't touch a basketball for several weeks, drowning in disappointment and what-ifs. But just like in the game, I wasn't alone. My teammates, my brothers, pulled me back in, encouraging me to step onto the court again, to move forward. That's when I realized that whether on the court or in life, grief is not meant to be carried alone. Healing comes in the presence of others, in the support of those who refuse to let us stay on the bench forever.

The buzzer had sounded, but the game wasn't over. Overtime stretched the night longer than expected, testing the endurance of every player on the court. Some fans sat on the edge of their seats, willing their team to push through, while others struggled to believe the game was still going. That's how prolonged grief can feel—like an endless overtime, where the world expects you to move on, but your heart is still caught in the game you lost.

Prolonged Grief Disorder (PGD), recognized by the American Psychiatric Association, occurs when the deep pain of loss doesn't ease with time, interfering with daily life for more than a year. Unlike the natural waves of sadness that come and go, PGD can make people feel trapped in their grief, unable to re-engage with life. Dr. Katherine Shear, a leading expert in grief therapy, describes it as "a persistent form of intense grief in which yearning and longing for the deceased dominate a person's emotional life." Like a player stuck in the same play over and over, those experiencing PGD find it difficult to move forward, no matter how much time has passed.

But just as no championship is won alone, healing from prolonged grief requires a team. Researchers emphasize the role of community in navigating loss. Resilience is not about avoiding grief, but it is as Psychiatrist George Bonanno, author of The Other Side of Sadness, suggests it is "having the support and inner resources to endure it." Teammates in grief, whether family, friends, or support groups, help pass the ball when exhaustion sets in. They remind the grieving person that they don't have to carry the weight of loss alone.

Overtime in basketball can feel like forever, but the game does end. The same is true of grief. While the pain may never fully disappear, it can become part of a larger story—one where love, support, and small steps forward lead to healing. No one wins alone. Just like athletes don't win championships alone, mourners need others to carry them through.

The game had been over for weeks, but one player still sat on the bench, staring at the empty court. His teammates had moved forward, reviewing plays, preparing for the next challenge, but he remained stuck in the moment of loss, unable to shake the pain of defeat. Grief can hold a person in place the same way. While everyone around them seems to be finding their way forward, some struggle to step back into life. Recognizing when grief has become too heavy to bear alone is crucial. Signs such as persistent sadness, withdrawal from loved ones, difficulty performing daily tasks, or an overwhelming sense of hopelessness may indicate that someone needs additional support.

Seeking help is not a sign of weakness; it is a strategy for healing. Dr. Alan Wolfelt, a renowned grief counselor, reminds us that "mourning is not meant to be done alone; it requires witness. Healing happens when we allow others to walk with us." Therapy provides a safe space to explore deep emotions, while support groups remind people that they are not alone in their pain. Faith-based counseling, rooted in biblical wisdom, offers comfort and spiritual reassurance. Proverbs 11:14 (NKJV) affirms the power of guidance: "Where there is no counsel, the people fall; but in the multitude of counselors there is safety." Sometimes, healing begins when we let someone else help carry the burden.

For many, faith is a lifeline when grief feels unbearable. Jesus himself promised comfort to the brokenhearted, saying in *Matthew 5:4* (NKJV), "Blessed are those who mourn, for they shall be comforted." Churches and faith communities can provide structured support through grief ministries, pastoral counseling, and prayer groups. Having a place to share sorrow in the presence of compassionate believers can be the key to moving forward. Support doesn't always mean answers. It means presence, a reminder that even in the depths of grief, no one has to walk alone.

Just as no player can win a game single-handedly, no one should be expected to overcome grief without support. When someone is struggling beyond what is typical, their team—family, friends, church, and professionals—must step in. Galatians 6:2 (NKJV) calls us to this mission: "Bear one another's burdens and so fulfill the law of Christ." Healing is a shared effort, and sometimes, the strongest thing a grieving person can do is reach out a hand and let someone else pull them back into the game of life.

References

American Psychiatric Association. (2022). *Diagnostic and statistical manual of mental disorders* (5th ed., text rev.; DSM-5-TR). https://doi.org/10.1176/appi.books.9780890425787

Bonanno, G. A. (2009). *The other side of sadness: What the new science of bereavement tells us about life after loss*. Basic Books.

Shear, M. K. (2015). Complicated grief. *The New England Journal of Medicine, 372*(2), 153–160. https://doi.org/10.1056/NEJMcp1315618

Wolfelt, A. D. (2004). *Understanding your grief: Ten essential touchstones for finding hope and healing your heart*. Companion Press.

Chapter 9:

INVISIBLE GRIEF; THE HOME RUN CLEARED THE FENCE, BUT WE STILL LOST

When I was twelve years old, I played for the Royals in our local Little League. That summer, our team faced off against the Giants in what *The Daily News Journal* headlined as "Fearless Fred vs. Dandy Dan in a Pitcher's Duel." I'll never forget it. In the top of the final inning, I hit a solo home run over the right field fence—my first ever. The bench erupted. I jogged the bases, beaming, sure that we'd clinched the win. My teammates slapped my helmet as I returned to the dugout. But in the bottom half, Dandy Dan—our rival's star—hit a two-run homer. They won the game. I walked off the field heartbroken. That was my first significant lesson in losing in playing organized sport: not the kind that involves funerals or final goodbyes, but the kind that sneaks in through disappointment, change, or dashed expectations.

As I've grown older and sat with others through their grief, I've come to understand that *not all grief is about death*. Sometimes we grieve the loss of a marriage, the end of a friendship, a dream deferred, or even something as seemingly simple as moving away. These losses may not bring casseroles or condolence cards, but they cut just as deeply. Psychologists refer to these experiences as "ambiguous loss," a term coined by Dr. Pauline Boss. She suggests that "ambiguous loss defies closure" and often leaves people in emotional limbo, unsure how to process the pain (Boss, 2006). And yet, grief is real even when there's no obituary or funeral.

One of the most jarring non-death losses people faces is divorce or the end of a long-term relationship. The breaking of a covenant, whether legal, emotional, or spiritual, can trigger grief as profound as bereavement. The routines you once shared, the plans for the future, the identity you built as a couple, all vanish. According to the Holmes and Rahe Stress Scale, divorce ranks second only to the death of a spouse in terms of life stressors (Holmes & Rahe, 1967). The heart mourns what could've been, even while the world keeps turning.

Then there are the losses that creep in through aging and diminishing independence. I remember the day my siblings and I had to take the car keys from our mother. She had always been fiercely independent. Driving wasn't just transportation; it was freedom. But as her mobility declined, so did her reaction time and confidence on the road. We knew it was time, but she didn't agree. That conversation was a quiet kind of heartbreak, for her, and for us. She was not a happy camper. And to be honest, I wasn't either. That day, we all grieved the loss of control, autonomy, and the shifting roles in our family. It's been several years since that eventful reality of mother's reduced independence, and she longingly mentions wanting to drive from time to time.

Moving away from a familiar community can be another form of grief. I've counseled people who moved for jobs or to care for aging parents, only to feel isolated, invisible, or unmoored in the new place. Though we don't often label this grief, it fits all the criteria: a deep sense of loss, emotional pain, disorientation, and the slow journey of adjustment. "Grief is the conflicting feelings caused by the end of or change in a familiar pattern of behavior," says John James and Russell Friedman in *The Grief Recovery Handbook* (2009). Leaving behind your support system, routines, and even your favorite coffee shop can activate sorrow that feels out of proportion—until you name it for what it is: grief.

The grieving process for these kinds of losses follows a similar arc to bereavement. Denial, anger, bargaining, depression, and acceptance, the familiar stages proposed by Elisabeth Kübler-Ross, still show up, although not always in order or at predictable times. More recent research suggests that grief is not linear. Instead, it ebbs and flows like waves. Some days are high tide, others mercifully calm. What's key is that we give ourselves permission to feel it, name it, and walk through it, preferably not in isolation.

Dealing with non-death losses requires intentional strategies. Journaling, therapy, support groups, spiritual direction, and even physical activities like walking or gardening can help create space for healing. Naming the loss, finding community, and choosing rituals, even small ones, can provide meaning and movement. For some, writing a goodbye letter to the life they're leaving behind is a powerful practice. For others, acknowledging the change in prayer or lighting a candle becomes a sacred pause in the chaos. "Harvard Health Publishing (2021) emphasizes that acknowledging and processing grief—even one that isn't tied to death — is important for preventing prolonged stress and supporting emotional and physical well-being." In grief, symbol and support matter, even when the loss is "invisible" to others.

I often go back to that Little League game. I remember the crack of the bat, the brief glory of my solo homer, and the hollow silence after Dan's final swing. I had to grieve that game. Not because it was epic, but because it meant something to me. In the same way, our everyday heartbreaks matter. "The Lord is close to the brokenhearted and saves those who are crushed in spirit" (Psalm 34:18, NIV). Jesus Himself said, "Blessed are those who mourn, for they shall be comforted" (Matthew 5:4). Whether it's the death of a loved one or the end of an era, God meets us there. Author Brené Brown puts it this way: "Grief requires us to reorient ourselves the pieces of ourselves that were shattered by loss." I went on to play more baseball by moving from Little League to Babe Ruth the next summer.

REFERENCES

Boss, P. (2006). *Loss, Trauma, and Resilience: Therapeutic Work with Ambiguous Loss*. W.W. Norton & Company.

Brown, B. (2015). *Rising Strong*. Spiegel & Grau.

Harvard Health Publishing. (2021). *Grieving nondeath losses during the pandemic*. Harvard Medical School. https://www.health.harvard.edu/mind-and-mood/grieving-nondeath-losses-during-the-pandemic

Holmes, T. H., & Rahe, R. H. (1967). *The Social Readjustment Rating Scale. Journal of Psychosomatic Research*, 11(2), 213–218.

James, J., & Friedman, R. (2009). *The Grief Recovery Handbook: The Action Program for Moving Beyond Death, Divorce, and Other Losses*. HarperCollins.

Kübler-Ross, E. (1969). *On Death and Dying*. Macmillan.

The Holy Bible, New International Version. (2011). Biblica. (Psalm 34:18; Matthew 5:4)

Chapter 10:

THE CHAMPIONSHIP – FINDING MEANING AND MOVING FORWARD

The 2007 New York Giants knew adversity well. They had stumbled through the regular season, finishing with ten wins but never being seen as true contenders. When the playoffs arrived, they weren't given much of a chance. Every game would be on the road, every opponent a giant, and at every turn, doubt hovered over them like a thick fog. But inside that locker room, there was no fear, only belief. They leaned on each other, battle-tested warriors who had been bruised and beaten but never broken. Grief, much like football, was a team sport, and this team had learned how to carry the weight together.

By the time they reached Super Bowl XLII, they stood face to face with history itself. The undefeated New England Patriots, a juggernaut destined for immortality. The world saw the Giants as nothing more than a footnote, but they saw themselves as something greater: a band of brothers who had survived the grind of the season, who had won when no one expected them to, and who had endured together. And when the moment came, when Eli Manning spun away from defenders, when David Tyree pinned the ball to his helmet, when Michael Strahan and Justin Tuck battered Tom Brady into submission, they proved that resilience isn't just about surviving the struggle. It's about embracing it.

For weeks after his father's passing, James found himself stuck between two worlds—one filled with memories of his father's laughter, the other with the hollow silence his absence left behind. He feared that moving forward meant leaving his father behind, that healing would somehow betray the love they shared. But then he read the words of

C.S. Lewis, who once wrote, "No one ever told me that grief felt so like fear." James realized that his fear wasn't of forgetting, but of facing the unknown without the man who had always been his guide. Healing, he slowly understood, wasn't about letting go of his father. It was about carrying him forward in a new way.

Honoring the deceased while moving forward is not about erasing their presence but weaving their memory into the fabric of our daily lives. Psychologist William Worden, known for his Four Tasks of Mourning, suggests that one must "find an enduring connection with the deceased while embarking on a new life." James began to do this in small ways, wearing his father's watch, telling his children bedtime stories the way his father once did, and continuing their tradition of Saturday morning walks. These rituals didn't trap him in the past; they allowed him to bring his father's spirit into the future.

Philosopher Søren Kierkegaard once wrote, "Life can only be understood backwards; but it must be lived forwards." It was a truth James clung to as he navigated the tension between remembering and rebuilding. He learned that moving forward didn't mean closing the door on grief; it meant carrying love with him into new experiences. He found solace in service, in sharing his father's wisdom with others, and in speaking his name often, ensuring that his legacy wasn't confined to the past but infused into the present.

In time, James discovered what author Mitch Albom expressed so well: "Death ends a life, not a relationship." His father's physical presence was gone, but his influence remained—alive in the lessons he had passed down, in the stories that were still being told, and in the love that could never be erased. Moving forward was no longer an act of leaving behind; it was an act of carrying forward. And like any great team, James realized that grief was not meant to be endured alone. It was meant to be shared, supported, and transformed into something that allowed love to live on.

For months after losing my brother, Ernest, during COVID, I wrestled with the weight of grief, unsure of how to move forward. The loss felt too vast, too final, as if the world had shifted beneath my feet and left me unsteady. But in the quiet moments of reflection, supported by family and therapeutic pastoral friends, I realized something—grief and recovery, while deeply personal, were not meant to be carried alone. It was meant to be transformed, shaped into something that honored Ernie's life rather than just mourning his absence. That realization planted a seed, one that would sprout resilience and grow into purpose, the writing of this book.

Psychologist William Worden, in his *Four Tasks of Mourning*, describes the final task as "finding an enduring connection with the deceased while embarking on a new life." Knowing that keeping Ernie's memory alive didn't mean staying stuck in sorrow. It meant turning my loss into something meaningful. Some people find that purpose in volunteering, serving in ways that reflect the values of their loved ones. Others become advocates, speaking out on issues that affect those they lost. For me, the path became clear: I should write, sharing my journey of grief in a way that could help others navigate their losses.

Forging new traditions became another way to carry Ernie's legacy forward. Instead of letting the holidays become a painful reminder of who was missing, I have chosen to celebrate Ernie and others so dear to me by telling how he rescued me from rescued me from the grips of Tommy Climber while playing king of the mountain in elementary school and being grateful to God for the time we had together. Dr. Alan Wolfelt, a grief expert, emphasizes that "mourning is not about 'getting over it' but about integrating loss into our lives." These traditions weren't about replacing the past; they were about creating new ways to feel connected to my brother.

Writing this book has become both a personal journey and a way to help others. Author Joan Didion once wrote, "We tell ourselves stories in order to live." I found healing by putting my grief into words, knowing that through these pages, Ernie's story would continue. Grief had taken something from me, but it had also given me something, a calling. And as I moved forward, I carried the lesson that grief is never meant to be endured in isolation. It is a team effort, one where love, remembrance, and purpose can turn loss into legacy. "You cannot afford to let grief define you. Let it refine you," says Eric Thomas. Resilience emerges when individuals turn their pain into purpose.

When Lisa, a work acquaintance, lost her husband unexpectedly, the world around her seemed to collapse. The mornings were the hardest, waking up to the empty space beside her, the quiet absence of his laughter. For weeks, she withdrew, convinced that no one could truly understand the depth of her pain. But then, her church family stepped in. They didn't try to fix her grief or offer empty platitudes. Instead, they simply showed up, bringing meals, sitting with her in silence, praying over her when words failed. One day, her pastor reminded her of Isaiah 41:10: "Fear not, for I am with you; be not dismayed, for I am your God; I will strengthen you, I will help you, I will uphold you with my righteous right hand." It was through this unwavering support that Lisa found the strength to keep going, one small step at a time.

For Marcus, the death of his best friend in a car accident nearly shattered him. They had grown up together, played football side by side, and dreamed of running a business together. Without him, Marcus felt lost. But his teammates, his lifelong friends, rallied around him. They encouraged him to keep training, channeling his grief into action. One of them handed him a book on grief with a handwritten note inside: "We're in this together. You don't have to carry this alone." Inspired by their support, Marcus decided to honor his friend by mentoring young athletes, teaching them not just about the game but about resilience, teamwork, and perseverance. As Romans 8:28 says, "And we know that all things work together for good to those who love God." Slowly, Marcus saw that even in his pain, purpose could be born. Eric Thomas states, "Your pain is a part of your prize, your struggle is a part of your story." Embracing growth through pain allows individuals to reclaim their power and purpose.

Eleanor had been married for forty-two years when she lost her husband to cancer. For months, the loneliness was unbearable. But one sunny morning, an elderly woman at church took her hands and whispered, "You still have so much love to give." That simple statement changed everything. Eleanor began volunteering at a local hospice, offering comfort to others facing loss. In giving, she found healing. Viktor Frankl, a Holocaust survivor and psychiatrist, once wrote, "When we are no longer able to change a situation, we are challenged to change ourselves." Eleanor discovered that while she couldn't bring her husband back, she could transform her grief into love for those who needed it most.

Grief is a team sport—and no one heals from loss by sitting on the sidelines. Every story in this book reminds us that grief isn't meant to be faced solo. Like any great team, we win by leaning on each other. *Ecclesiastes 4:9-10* says, "Two are better than one... If either of them falls down, one can help the other up." In the toughest seasons, our teammates show up: family passes the ball of comfort, friends play defense against despair, and faith keeps us grounded when the score feels lopsided. Resilience isn't pretending the pain's not there, it's learning how to play through it. We don't move on from grief; we move forward with it, supported by those running beside us. *Psalm 23:4* assures us that even in the darkest valley, our divine Coach walks with us, calling the plays and giving us strength. So, we huddle up. We pray. We pass hope down the line. And we press on—together. Grief may change the game, but with the right team, we can still claim victory. Let's win—side by side.

REFERENCE LIST

Albom, M. (2003). *The five people you meet in heaven.* Hyperion.

Didion, J. (1979). "The White Album." In The White Album.

Frankl, V. E. (2006). *Man's search for meaning* (I. Lasch, Trans.). Beacon Press. (Original work published 1946)

Kierkegaard, S. (1964). *Journals and papers* (H. V. Hong & E. H. Hong, Eds.). Indiana University Press.

Lewis, C. S. (1961). *A grief observed.* Faber & Faber.

The Holy Bible, English Standard Version. (2001). Crossway Bibles. (Original work published 2001)

Worden, J. W. (2009). *Grief counseling and grief therapy: A handbook for the mental health practitioner* (4th ed.). Springer Publishing Company.

Wolfelt, A. D. (2004). *Understanding your grief: Ten essential touchstones for finding hope and healing your heart.* Companion Press.

ABOUT THE AUTHOR

Fred Batten, Jr., DMin
Speaker • Author • Pastor • Chaplain

Dr. Fred Batten, Jr. is a trusted voice in grief recovery and spiritual resilience. With over 25 years of leadership, ministry, and chaplaincy experience, he has guided countless individuals and communities through life's most painful moments. Certified by the John Maxwell Team in leadership development, Dr. Batten combines heartfelt wisdom with practical strategies to help others heal, grow, and move forward with purpose.

Dr. Batten is also the author of *Wisdom from Generation to Generation*, a reflective work on thriving across life's seasons. His voice continues to inspire individuals, families, and faith communities to face life's deepest valleys with courage, compassion, and hope.

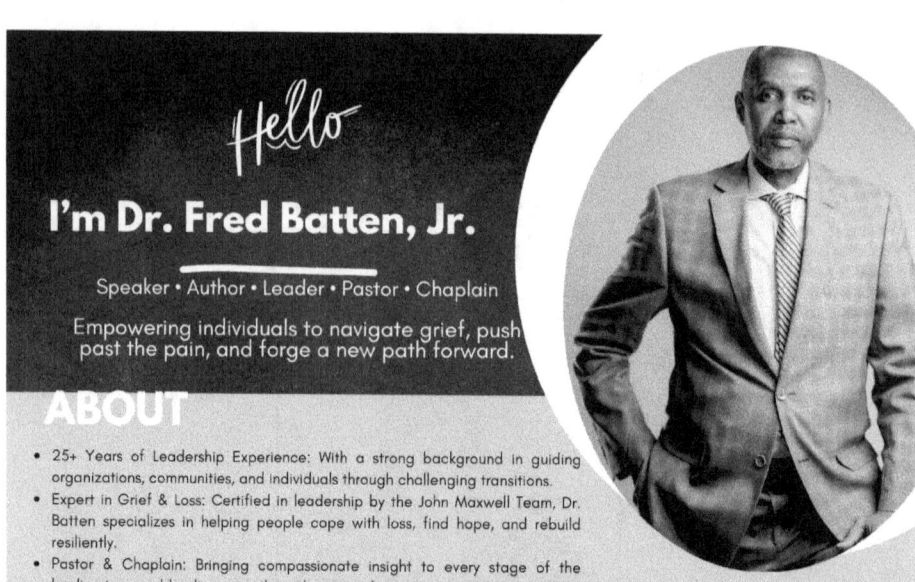

Hello

I'm Dr. Fred Batten, Jr.

Speaker • Author • Leader • Pastor • Chaplain

Empowering individuals to navigate grief, push past the pain, and forge a new path forward.

ABOUT

- 25+ Years of Leadership Experience: With a strong background in guiding organizations, communities, and individuals through challenging transitions.
- Expert in Grief & Loss: Certified in leadership by the John Maxwell Team, Dr. Batten specializes in helping people cope with loss, find hope, and rebuild resiliently.
- Pastor & Chaplain: Bringing compassionate insight to every stage of the healing journey, blending empathy with practical strategies.
- Author: His book, Wisdom from Generation to Generation, offers timeless insights and and actionable advice for thriving across life's seasons.

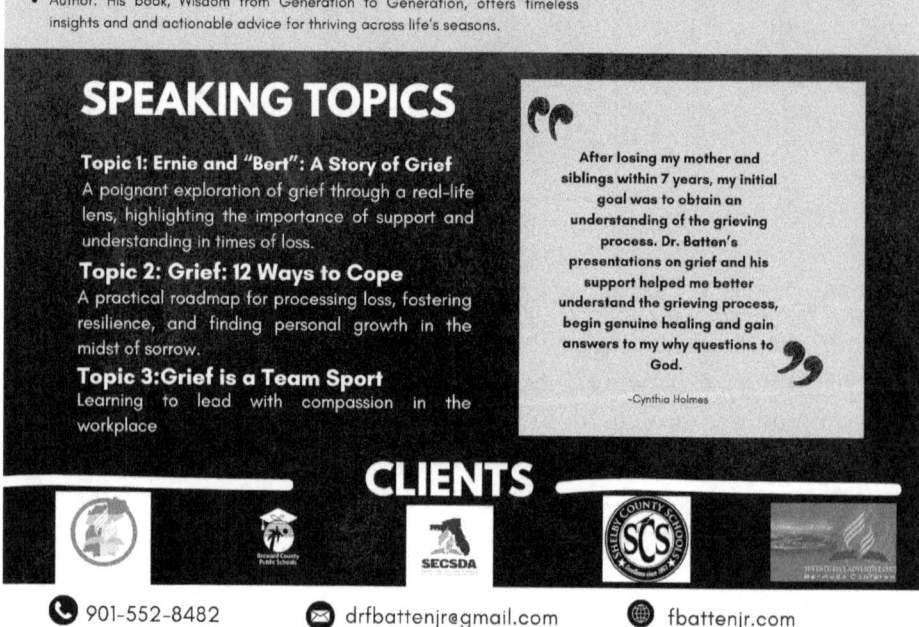

SPEAKING TOPICS

Topic 1: Ernie and "Bert": A Story of Grief
A poignant exploration of grief through a real-life lens, highlighting the importance of support and understanding in times of loss.

Topic 2: Grief: 12 Ways to Cope
A practical roadmap for processing loss, fostering resilience, and finding personal growth in the midst of sorrow.

Topic 3: Grief is a Team Sport
Learning to lead with compassion in the workplace

After losing my mother and siblings within 7 years, my initial goal was to obtain an understanding of the grieving process. Dr. Batten's presentations on grief and his support helped me better understand the grieving process, begin genuine healing and gain answers to my why questions to God.

-Cynthia Holmes

CLIENTS

Broward County Public Schools

SECSDA

SHELBY COUNTY SCHOOLS SCS

📞 901-552-8482   ✉ drfbattenjr@gmail.com   🌐 fbattenjr.com

The *Grief is a Team Sport Workbook* can be used in conjuction with this book.

Available in paperback.

ISBN: 978-1-964972-16-9

www.ingramcontent.com/pod-product-compliance
Lightning Source LLC
Chambersburg PA
CBHW061715120626
46550CB00003B/1232